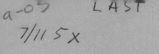

How Things Grow

From Egg

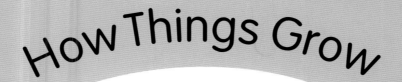

to Duck

Sally Morgan

Thameside Press

Distributed in the United States by
Smart Apple Media
1980 Lookout Drive
North Mankato, MN 56003

Text by Sally Morgan

ISBN 1-930643-86-1

Library of Congress Control Number 2002 141387

Series editor: Jean Coppendale
Designer: Angie Allison
Picture researchers: Sally Morgan and Terry Forshaw
Consultant: Bethan Currenti

Printed in Hong Kong

10 9 8 7 6 5 4 3 2 1

Picture acknowlededements:
All photography Chrysalis Images/Robert Pickett with the exception of:
Front cover (main) & 5 Papilio; 4 Pictor International; 10 Kintaline Poultry & Wildfowl
Centre, Benderloch, Oban, Argyll, www.domesticducks.co.uk; 15 & back cover (L)
PowerstockZefa; 19 Swift Imagery/Pauline J. Thornton; 20 FLPA/Foto
Natura Stock/D. Ellinger; 21 Ecoscene/Gryniewicz; 22 Papilio/Steve Austin; 23
(T) Ecoscene/Angela Hampton, (B) Ecoscene/Anthony Cooper; 24
Ecoscene/Ian Beames; 25 & front cover (inset) Ecoscene/Paul
Ferraby; 26 & back cover (R) Papilio; 27 Ecoscene/Anthony Cooper.

Contents

What is a duck?

A duck is a type of bird. Its body is covered in feathers and it has two wings for flying. Ducks live near ponds, lakes, and rivers.

A duck has a long body and short legs.

4

A duck has
a long, wide beak.
It pushes its beak into water,
mud, and grass to find food.

Ducks **waddle**
over land, but they
are most at home on water. They
love to paddle and dive underwater.
Their **webbed** feet help them to walk
over muddy ground and swim.

5

Spring arrives

In spring, the ducks and drakes form pairs and mate.

Male ducks are called **drakes**. A duck and a drake form a pair and **mate**. A female duck builds a nest made from straw, leaves, and twigs. She lines the inside of the nest with feathers from her body.

Ducks start to lay their eggs in spring. They know it is time to start egg-laying when the days become longer and warmer. The duck lays one egg every two days, until there are about ten eggs in the nest.

The eggs in a nest are called a **clutch**.

The egg

A duck egg has a tough shell. The shell protects the duckling inside. Inside the egg is a yellow **yolk**. This is surrounded by a clear jelly called the egg white.

The shell of the egg is very hard and difficult to break.

The egg yolk
fills up most
of the egg. It
is surrounded
by egg white.

A tiny **embryo** lies on the yolk.
This embryo will grow into a
duckling. The egg yolk supplies
the embryo with food.

Keeping warm

The duck sits on her nest all day. She only gets up to eat and drink.

When the duck has laid all her eggs, she sits on them for 28 days. She keeps the eggs warm. This is called **incubation**. Every few hours, she turns the eggs over using her beak.

After 20 days, the duckling fills more than half the egg. The yellow egg yolk is much smaller.

Inside the egg, the duckling is growing. The yolk gets smaller as the food is used up. After 28 days, the duckling fills up almost all of the egg. Tiny peeps can be heard coming from the egg. The duckling is ready to hatch.

After 28 days, the duckling is fully-grown. Its wings and legs are folded so they take up less space. All of the yolk has gone.

11

Time to hatch

The duckling has to break through the eggshell. It has a special tooth on the top of its beak called an egg tooth. The duckling uses its egg tooth to break the shell from the inside.

First, a tiny crack appears in the eggshell.

Then, the duckling pushes its egg tooth against the shell to make the crack bigger.

12

The duckling
pushes hard
with its legs and
the shell splits
open. The head and
wings appear first,
followed by the legs.

The duckling has
just hatched. Its
feathers are
wet, but they
will soon
dry out.

Following mom

A duckling can stand up and run only an hour after hatching. It huddles under its mother with all the other ducklings. The ducklings stay close to their mother and run to her side when she calls.

A duckling has fluffy yellow feathers. It can see and call out to its mother.

They quickly learn to recognize their mother's shape and they follow her everywhere. The duck keeps a look out for **predators** who may eat her ducklings.

A mother duck checks for danger before leading her ducklings to water.

Growing up

The ducklings grow quickly. Their fluffy feathers are replaced by stiff white feathers. Ducks eat plants, slugs, and snails.

This three-week-old duckling still has a few fluffy feathers. Long, stiff feathers are growing on its tail.

Ducks use their large beaks to scoop-up food from the ground and **dabble** in the mud. Ducks have webbed feet with toes that end in tiny claws. Their large feet help them to walk over mud and swim underwater.

By six weeks, the ducklings have grown a set of new feathers. They still follow their parents.

17

Feathers

Small down feathers (1) help to keep the duck warm. A contour feather is smaller and soft (2). A flight feather is long and stiff (3).

A duck's body is covered in feathers. The feathers keep the duck warm and dry. There are different types of feather. Each type has a different job. The long, stiff feathers on the wing and tail are used for flying.

Most of a duck's body is covered with smaller, soft feathers. These are called **contour feathers**. They give the duck a smooth outline or shape. The smallest feathers are the **down feathers**. They are close to the duck's skin.

Ducks spend much of the day keeping their feathers clean. This is called **preening**. They spread oil over their feathers to make them **waterproof**.

Long winter

Feathers and fat help to keep a duck warm during snowy weather.

In the fall, the older ducks lose some of their old feathers. This is called **molting**. The old feathers are replaced by bright new ones. Ducks eat a lot of food in summer. They build up a layer of fat under their skin.

Ducks need this fat in winter when the ground is hard and may even be covered by snow. The ducks may not be able to find food then. The fat provides them with food and helps to keep them warm.

Icy weather makes it hard for ducks and other birds to find food.

Finding a partner

Some male and female ducks look the same. So how can you tell them apart? The male, or drake, has curled feathers at the end of its tail. A female duck has straight tail feathers.

A drake has small, curled feathers at the end of his tail.

This pair of ducks are about to start bobbing their heads up and down.

The mallard drake has colorful feathers. The mallard duck is dull brown.

Ducks can quack but drakes cannot. When a duck is ready to breed, it has to find a partner. Before they mate, ducks and drakes do a dance. They stand together and bob their heads up and down.

Life span

The red fox hunts and kills birds, including ducks.

Many weak or sick ducks are killed by predators. Ducklings may be killed by a large fish called a pike. The pike hides in the shadows in the water and grabs the duckling from below as it swims by.

A pet duck may live for 20 years or more. But a wild duck may live for only four or five years. As ducks grow older, they lay fewer eggs.

People often keep ducks in pens to protect them from foxes and other predators.

The duck family

There are
many types of ducks.
The largest members of the duck family are swans and geese. All of these birds live near water and have webbed feet. One of the most colorful ducks is the Mandarin duck. The male Mandarin has bright orange feathers.

The mute swan builds a huge nest in which the female lays about seven eggs. She sits on her eggs for 36 days. The young swans are called cygnets and they are born with gray feathers.

Swans run over the surface of the water, beating their wings to take off.

The life cycle

1 A duck lays its eggs in a nest made from leaves, straw, and twigs.

2 The egg is protected by a hard shell. Inside there is a yellow egg yolk and a clear egg white.

7 After a few weeks, the fluffy feathers are replaced by long stiff feathers.

8 When the duck is a few years old, it finds a partner and mates.

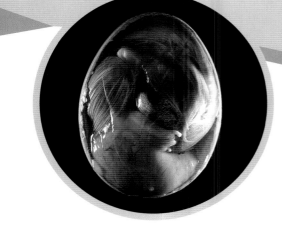

3 The duckling grows inside the egg. It feeds on the egg yolk.

4 After 28 days, the duckling is ready to hatch. It pecks its way out of the eggshell.

6 The duckling feeds on seeds, plants, and insects. It grows very quickly.

5 The duckling can stand up and run around soon after hatching.

Glossary

clutch   A batch of eggs laid by a bird.

contour feathers   Feathers which cover the body of a bird and give it a smooth shape.

dabble   To move the beak and feet around in water or mud.

down feathers   The tiny, soft feathers close to a bird's skin. A duck pulls out her downy feathers to line her nest.

drakes   Male ducks.

embryo   The young of an animal at very early stages of development.

incubation   Keeping eggs warm until they hatch. Most birds incubate their eggs by sitting on them.

mate   To pair or breed.

molting   Losing old feathers and growing new ones.

predators   Animals that hunt and kill other animals for food.

preening   When a bird cleans its feathers.

waddle   Walk with short steps, swaying from side to side.

waterproof   Not allowing water to pass through.

webbed   Having a flap of skin between each toe.

yolk   The food store of an egg.